Surviving the Great Recession

J.P. Johnson

Editor

Melissa Landon

Photographer

Sean Polhemus

ISBN-13: 978-0615730790

ISBN-10: 0615730795

johnsonjp34@msn.com

Table of Contents

Introduction

It doesn't take a rocket scientist to convince you that the economies of the world are struggling, and even in America, it appears as if there is no hope in sight. The rather appropriate term "Great Recession" is frequently used in the home to describe the turn in financial mood that began in 2008. Recent college grads, senior members of the workforce, and even those self-employed all blame their loss of income on the Great Recession.

What is a person to do to establish a firm financial basis in these uncertain times? Is it possible? Does one have to change his entire lifestyle? I will attempt to tackle these questions in the next hour and even provide some practical methods available to all to get the financial ship back in order.

This is not a get-rich-quick scheme or a self-motivation guide but rather a text that encourages hard work and discipline to achieve a desired lifestyle. We have all heard the fundamentals of finance, but we often choose to quietly ignore them, and as a result, we suffer the consequences. I will present these fundamentals in a manner that doesn't seem out of touch with reality, and if embraced will allow you to achieve your financial goals.

Chapter 1 The American Situation

An important edit to make to the American mentality is that it is possible for economic conditions to worsen. As a financial advisor, I am often asked how low a particular stock could drop. Rarely do I reply with anything other than *goose egg*. Zero is always possible, and when handling life, regardless of your personal risk tolerance, always keep in mind that things can get worse. As we move through life, there is always a cloud hovering over our heads that could potentially bring rain or even hail. As depressing as such a notion is, we must embrace the attitude that our current lifestyle and income may be subject to change as a result of variables exceeding the number of grains of sand on the beach. After accepting this notion, we are free to move on to the strategic planning of our lives and resources to obtain or preserve the lifestyle we all wish for.

Perhaps financial destruction starts at an early age. Assuming any level of education or job skill will land you a lifetime career is a myth and must be immediately exterminated.

Education doesn't equal a career and job skills don't equal a career. These methods can increase the likelihood of finding a decent job, but there is no certificate of guarantee with any sort of schooling that promises you your dream job or its permanence. Often times I see parents telling their children that college is the end all start to life. Parents lead their children to believe that sitting in a classroom for four years will earn them a high-paying job. Statistics do show that attending post-secondary programs increase the lifetime wages of the individual. ONE problem with this thought process, though, is that it appears that almost all people now are seeking higher education. As American institutions are pushing out college graduates like a paperclip factory, the workforce pool is becoming more and more saturated with applicants with just another degree.

This is disturbing because debt loads are increasing while unemployment numbers continue to remain elevated. Many students struggle to pay off their college bills and can barely keep up with putting food on the table or paying rent. I am not discouraging the pursuit of education and/or new job skills, but I want to clarify that just as there is the possibility that times could get worse, making large educational investments may produce even more financial hardship.

Continuing this line of depressing and myth debunking thought is the prospect of job security. Twenty-first century job security has, in my mind, reached the list of Oxy Moron's funniest. Consider the once well-established and previously held as blue chip manufacturing companies such as Ford, General Motors, or even Cincinnati Milacron. At various points in their existence many would have safely assumed that their jobs were safe, and were, as I hate to mention it , Titanic proof. In this highly competitive and often cut-throat job market, survival of the fittest has become the new dogma.

As people, we love to spend what we earn and often more than we earn. Upon loss of a job or disability, will you be able to sustain meeting current expenses and lifestyle at least until you find another income source at the same level? I will not engage in a discourse on all the reasons not to over-extend credit and why you should put money away for downturns. We all have been taught to save, but it never seems to happen. At this point, I want you just to keep the thought in mind that your job is not permanent. At anytime it could easily disappear like a drop of gasoline on a hot summer day. When we put these notions of security away, we are able to plan safeguards to prevent future financial disruption.

Chapters 2-4 will focus on how to take charge of your finances, how to get the sinking finance ship back in order, and how to build confidence in your financial status. Chapters 5-9 will discuss real world and practical activities you can use as a source of supplemental income. These supplemental income sources are based upon the fabrics that seem to hold our society together in this tech age. Topics include understanding Ebay as a tool, understanding the Rental Property Model, finding your niche in the part-time skilled labor market, using your computer to generate dollars, and finally converting a favorite hobby into a profitable venture. Chapter 10 will focus on the long-term financial outlook and how to prepare for retirement. All of these chapters are constructed as a guide to be referenced.

Chapter 2 Taking Charge of Your Finances

Impending financial doom is certainly something we all are striving for. Wait, what? Financial apathy is at its greatest point in history. I hear it frequently said by people on the street that their retirement accounts are significantly down. When you ask them what is in their portfolio, typically you get this blank stare with a, "I have no idea." How many people even know how to do their own taxes? With many activities in life, what you put into life is what you will get out of it. Because one is not a financial professional doesn't mean he cannot make an effort to understand his financial situation. No financial planner, no advisor, no tax preparer, no accountant, no bank, no lending entity, no college, no insurance company, no car salesman, dare I continue, cares or has more control over your money than you do.

Would you put all of your money into a ziplock bag and hand it over to the first stranger you see on the street and ask them to take care of it? If you are a person tolerant of risk you would probably at least ask the stranger what he or she was going to do with the money. Do you know where all your money is going and why it is going there? My first bit of guidance to take control of your finances is to keep track of your expenses. With technology it is easy to download a free budget app to your smart phone or computer. Trust me, if you haven't tabled all of your expenses for a month, you are missing out on some valuable information that can tell you much about yourself and your family. If you are a first time budgeter you should tuck away all receipts and add them up at the end of the month or even use your credit or debit card to keep track of expenses at the end of the month. If you keep track of your expenses daily at the beginning you will probably encounter some psychological effect (of which the science I know nothing about) and end up spending a different quantity in the month had you not been keeping track. Divide total expenses at the end of the month into categories that you are familiar with such as housing, utilities, food, insurance, fuel, vehicle, pleasure, or whatever categories you feel are pertinent to your situation.

For many after totaling expenses a brief period of shock comes upon them. Even as a financial planner, I am often shocked to discover what I have been spending so much of my money on. Record keeping can become rather entertaining when you keep track of individual items such as Dunkin Donut consumption or the daily Starbucks run. I don't live anywhere near a Starbucks, but I still seem to manage to spend more than $30 a month at the coffee giant. At this point I am not condemning spending on any particular item or activity. You worked hard for your money, and you deserve to spend it however you choose.

After recording expenses the next step in the balancing act is determining the amount of income you have available. Looking at the top line of your salary can be very deceptive. Let's say Joe gets paid $50,000 a year, so he decides that he can safely spend $50,000 a year on whatever he wants. Of course we all know that the dreaded IRS and state and local governments want your money, too. I encourage you to look at the tax tables in the back of the 1040 booklet and see what percentage of your income is slated to just the federal government before adjustments. Keep in mind that sales tax, property tax, abc tax, def tax, ghi tax, etc, all add up, too, and greatly subtract from your buying power. (Useful income is what is left after Uncle Sam reaches into your pocket.)

When you have wrestled with the calculator for a couple hours and have determined your monthly expenses and your useful income, you can now determine a simple positive or negative number that represents whether you are spending more than you are making. Do not include the total cost of financed items such as a house or car for that year. Instead, subtract from your useful income the amount you have paid for that year. Credit cards, on the other hand, are a different story. Depending on interest rates, the amount borrowed, and the amount you continue to use your card, determining how much you are spending on this piece can be rather difficult. For simplicity's sake, determine on average, the amount charged that month if you believe it represents what you spend on an average month with the cards. Take this value and also subtract it from your useful income. Next, determine how much the monthly payments are for your credit cards and multiply this number by 1.5. Subtract this number from your useful income number. I use the multiply by 1.5 factor because we have all read on our credit card statements how many million years and dollars later it will take to pay those cards off if you only make the minimum payment. I believe, paying 1.5 times the minimum is not a maximum, but rather a minimum goal to reach.

When subtracting these numbers from the useful income, you can divide the useful income by 12 to determine useful income for the month, or you can just take your monthly expenses and multiply them by twelve for an estimate. Both methods have some slight problems as all expenses can't be accounted for in an estimate. Also, what you are making at the beginning of the year may not be an accurate representation of the entire year. If you haven't broken your calculator or hit your head against the desk yet, I congratulate you. If you find that your expenses are exceeding your income, this is an issue, but it isn't out of the American norm. I suggest that you run around your home five or six times screaming at the top of your lungs, "I'm broke." Okay. Don't do that. Calm down. Being in debt, going broke, or being broke aren't the worst things in the world, and stressing about them only makes things worse. The problem I often see is that people absolutely freak out when they see a financial cliff coming up. This stress prevents them from making objective decisions and often causes them to do things that may not be so wise. "I'm broke and terrible with money. Now what, go to the pawn shop and sell grandmas favorite pearl necklace?" I would hold off on that one and any other decision that you may regret down the road.

For those of you who came out with a positive number, good job at this point. Now ask yourself what would happen if my spouse or I suddenly could not work tomorrow. Is your number still positive? If so, again good job, you most certainly are on top of things. Many are in the positive category, but as we know, job loss could happen at anytime, and sickness or accidents in the family could cause sudden disruptions in the income stream. If little Johnny becomes severely injured, I guarantee that for me it would be a priority to be there for him instead of being at work. For many of us though, if we don't work, we don't get paid. Now what? This is where it becomes important to ensure that we have a method of keeping our income greater than our expenses. What stops do we have to put in place? What can I do now to prevent such a financial cliff? What do I do if I am already there? In chapter three, I will answer these questions. For now, put the calculator away and get ready to turn the page.

Chapter 3 Turning the Ship Around

When I recall the first time I ever attempted to paddle a two person kayak, I remember it seemed as if I were going in circles for the first half hour of the trip. Whenever multiple people are rowing, some sort of coordination is needed. I learned that course corrections are not as simple as they are on land such as in an automobile. Generally when we apply the brakes and turn the steering wheel, we receive an almost instantaneous response. This is not so much the case in the water. I remember attempting to stop the kayak. I placed the paddle in the water on one side; the kayak slowed down, but it also turned to that side as well. Finances behave more like a boat than an automobile. Decisions to change a given route have to be given in advance with plenty of time for the desired correction to come into play. Building a firm financial foundation is not something that will happen overnight; but rather it is a gradual process that requires firm and patient decision-making.

Now that we are in the boat, what is the first step to get on our way? Initially you must pick a destination. What do you want to do with your life? What are your priorities? At what point in our adventure are we to accomplish these goals? Once we determine that, we can tailor our expenditures to meet our needs and ambitions.

Pull out your expenditure sheet again and review the categories that you put in place to organize your expenses. Look at the items you purchased, invested time in, or just plain emptied your wallet on last month. Are they meaningful to you or do they seem like an expense and nothing more than an expense? What about those items in your expense list that are not necessary? Consider each item in your list and ask yourself if that expense was really worth to you and your family what it produced. While I do enjoy those trips to Starbucks, spending $5+ on some super-venti-americano-frappe-iced-tea-coffee-with-bacon is not necessary for my existence. I replaced these coffee runs with a simple coffee maker at home. Even though a few dollars a month doesn't seem like much, we have to consider the actual cost of our investments.

Everyone and his brother have heard of the lovely terms inflation and interest rates. Consider the price of a fountain drink at about any restaurant or at the vending machine. Let us assume that between the two you usually end up spending $1.50 for that gotta-drink-it-now Mt. Dew. At two times a day, say five times a week, that is $60 a month. Now, imagine that you took that money and invested in some good corporate bonds paying 8%, which is not out of the norm, and took that $60 a month for 30 years and saved it. You would end up with over $90,000 (compounded only annually). Again, I am not asking you to cut your favorite expenditures or even interests, but I want you to realize how much that pop or cigarette is costing you now and in the future. (For you Android users, there are a couple great apps that allow you to see how much your habit will cost you with time. I recommend *Habit Cost* and *Financial Essentials* both by Investor Direction.)

Another method I have found to reduce expenses rather effectively is by not shopping. As simple of an idea this is, it is the absolute truth. I can say that I have never made a trip to Wal-Mart without spending at least $50 per visit. Typically I need one item, usually $10 or less, but I come back with so much more stuff than I had planned. Don't worry; we all have done it, but what do we do about it? I recommend fewer trips to the store and making bigger purchases that are intended to take the place of multiple trips. Most big name retail chains are quite hypnotic and have labels on every product that scream, "PUT ME IN THE CART AND BUY ME NOW!!!" The less you have to expose yourself to such manipulation the better it will be for you and your family. In addition to this, you must consider the fuel and vehicle savings involved with less frequent shopping trips. Again, by no means become a hermit living off of your garden and homemade beef jerky, but keep in mind the psychology behind shopping.

Small leaks sink great ships. Another hole to patch up is the smart phone expense. Certain fruit and robot named devices make it extremely easy to purchase an infinite array of applications and other media at the touch of the finger. This on-demand media is certainly convenient and often useful. Bear in mind, though, that many have credit cards attached to those accounts, and frequent button pushing eventually adds up to a large some of money. It's the small leaks in combination that will sink the ship. Part of the problem with an almost purely digital monetary system is that people aren't as conscious of their money. In this tech world, we trade our invisible dollars for this and that at the touch of the screen. For many, I would dare say that if they had to insert a dollar or quarters every time they had to make an electronic purchase, they would feel the grief associated with letting their hard earned money go out the door for another silly ring tone. As I have stated so many times before, spending money is your fundamental right as an American, but it can just as easily become a fundamental burden to you and your family.

Vehicle expenses eat people whole without even using antacids. Consider a used car with a sticker price of $15,000 financed over five years at 5%. This produces a monthly payment of around $283. Now lets multiply this by 12 for a yearly payment of $3,396. Consider 15,000 miles per year traveled with a vehicle that averages 25 mpg and assume gas were to remain at $3.50. That is about $2,100 per year in fuel expenses for the one vehicle. Next, we must include insurance and repair costs which I will conservatively estimate at $1,500 per year, assuming nothing serious goes wrong with this vehicle. Add it all up, and now we have around $7000 per vehicle per year. These calculations are based upon a fairly inexpensive vehicle, decent fuel mileage, and a good financing interest rate. A person could easily spend $10,000-15,000 a year on one vehicle. At this point, we really haven't done anything wrong with owning this vehicle. I mean, this is a necessary requirement for most families in rural and suburban areas. What becomes rather hairy is that for many families the husband and the wife and the children all seem to want their own vehicles now. How much does one extra vehicle cost assuming it is constantly replaced as many Americans do over the course of say 30 years? Well, investing at 8%, this $7,000 over 30 years would yield $869,000. Eliminating an extra vehicle from the budget and cutting that daily beverage could remarkably alter your lifestyle at retirement time. Again, you have the freedom to spend your money as you wish, but you also have the option of taking that money you saved and build your dream home or whatnot.

So far, I have managed to avoid going into detail about those beloved credit cards. Before you go and cut up that plastic, I must cover the good side of cards and the responsibility of building a good credit score. The term credit has become a folly for many, a curse word for some, and a source of wealth for others. As it is with many ventures in life, your attitude and actions can make a credit card either a wonderful thing or a black hole. I encourage all young college students to at least have a few small college loans from the government and at least a couple credit cards. Why, so I can fall into a deep pit of debt despair? No, because building good credit is important in our world. You may be wealthy and debt-free, but you may still have to pay that deposit on next month's electric bill if you do not have established credit. Without a decent credit score, you cannot finance anything at a decent interest rate in this post financial fallout world.

A part of the credit score is actually based upon how long you have had credit accounts. Even if a 22-year-old opened an account when he turned 18 has paid every card on time for the last four years, he will not have a maxed out credit score. What about the 22-year-old who begins to establish credit by say, applying for a card after college graduation? It will take four years for that new college graduate (assuming payments are made on time and some other factors) to reach that credit score of the 22-year-old who began his credit history at high school graduation. This is a serious advantage in our credit world.

The 22-year-old who didn't have any college loans, will also be at a disadvantage. Even though most college loans do not require repayment during the education phase, if you check a credit report from the big three, you will see that every month a student is in school, he will receive good and constructive credit every month for doing absolutely nothing except having the loan(s). This is NOT permission to rack up an unacceptable quantity of debt, especially on the card side where rates can be in the 20% zone. I recommend keeping the balance on all cards low, as this makes them easier to pay off, and I also recommend setting these cards up on automatic pay at a rate higher than the minimum payment necessary so that you will not get into a debt trap, and you won't forget to make a payment on time each month.

For the crowd that went wild with spending and stacked up a sizable debt with high interest rates: relax. I am not going to point fingers of condemnation because we have all been in this position. The key to getting out of any bind, trap, hole, or trouble is to keep a clear head and systematically think your way out of the situation. First of all, gather all of your card statements and place them side-by-side. Carefully analyze each statement and determine the APR (annual percentage rate) of each credit card. Many have no idea what is being spent on interest charges. Legislation has required credit card companies to divulge how long it will take to pay that credit card off at the minimum payment level. Never make only minimum payments or it will seem to take a million years and a million dollars to pay that account off. Typing "credit card repayment" into Google you will find a page by the Federal Reserve that allows you to calculate the number of years it will take for repayment based upon your interest rate. There is also a nice calculator on the page that will allow you to determine how much you need to pay monthly to pay off the card in your desired time frame.

Just to kick you in the butt, I will input a simple example. Let us assume a $5000 credit card debt at a common 20% APR. How long will it take to pay this card off, and how much interest will end up being paid in the process at minimum payment levels? Using this nice calculator provided by our government, I entered the $5000 and 20% and determined that it would take 49 years to pay the debt and I would incur $21,169 of interest charges. Okay, someone grab the defibrillator. Is that even legal? It is, and too often people fall into that trap. There is a bright side, though. If you make more than the minimum payment, you can significantly decrease the number of years and incurred interest involved. For example, if I increased my monthly payment by only $33 dollars, I would be able to pay the card off in 5 years and only incur $2,949 in interest. Although that amount of interest is still intolerable, it is much better than $20,000+ over 49 years. I think we can all afford to put away the coffee and increase the amount paid towards our credit cards.

Continuing this interest rate game can be fun. If you are in a position where you can't make any more contributions to your cards in excess of the monthly payment, you may consider finding an outside source of funding such as a equity line of credit on your home or property. Although it is often not good to borrow more money, in this particular case it can become advantageous. If you can borrow money at, say, 6% and use that borrowed money to pay off your debt that is accumulating at 20%, I'd say it is an incredibly strong tool. Do not borrow from the equity in your home to buy stupid stuff. Another place that often allows for loans are 401(k) accounts. I do not recommend borrowing to pay off other debt unless the secondary loan contains a lower interest rate. Also, keep in mind that a loan against your home can cost you your home if you default. Not paying a credit card makes a bad credit report; a credit card is unsecured debt, so assets cannot be seized because you defaulted on the card.

If credit cards aren't enough for you to worry about let us talk about the Big D. Divorce is one of those issues you don't need statistics to prove that financial destruction can come from. Does ole Frank at the restaurant tell you every morning that she took the house, the kids, and left the bills? Perhaps it could be the other way around. I do recommend serious thought and prayer prior to marriage and to consider the potential financial consequences or advantages involved. What usually comes around after marriage? Babies and bigger cars right? All of a sudden a myriad of expenses just fell from the sky, and you have no idea what to do. Just remember, regardless of the situation, keeping a cool head and thinking through things is of great importance. Financial stress has been known to strain marriages and relationships. I recommend taking an active approach with the finances that involve the inclusion of you and your spouse in all matters. Not only does it reduce pressure knowing what the other is thinking, but also it can even be fun to strategically plan together where your money goes. I'm not asking you to have tightwad competitions with your spouse, but handling money should be fun and should be used to help keep the relationship together rather than split it apart.

If you are dying of cancer, work is probably the last thing on your mind. Terrible diseases happen all too often, but we never think it will happen to us or anyone in our families. We all want or have major medical insurance policies. Are they enough? I'm sure you have seen the coffee can by the register at the gas station or grocery store that has a picture of a young child or family suffering from a terminal disease and needs money. Even for major medical policies, there are always expenses and deductibles the insurance company won't pay no matter how sick you or your child is. What can we do about this? I seriously recommend analyzing your insurance plans to determine what your insurance covers and what it doesn't.

Can I afford that deductible? Can I afford treatment if it is outside of the network? What happens if I miss work for a day or for an extended period of time? You need to be able to answer these questions and provide a solution ensuring that you and your family are taken care of financially. When someone is hurt, the last thing you want on your mind is, "How am I going to pay for this?" I don't recommend supplemental policies to all (such as that quacking duck on TV), but it may be in your best interest if there are gaps in your major medical insurance. Also, if a supplemental line isn't right for you, I strongly encourage a savings account set aside just for medical associated expenses. Another option to consider is something similar to a Health Savings Account, which would allow you to save in a tax-favorable manner for a high-deductible insurance policy. This option may or may not be available to you. Check with your employer. Covering medical expenditures is always unique to the individual, and elaborating on every aspect of the complicated medical system is beyond this book, review your insurance policy, keep yourself informed, and develop solutions to problems before they occur.

Believe it or not, the previous few pages have provided a highlight of all the major financial holes in most lives. If you can navigate these waters, you will be well taken care of. Traversing these seas requires a specific mentality that I will cover in the next chapter.

Chapter 4 Confidence Building

You should handle your money with great pride. After all, it is your money and you earned it right? Being responsible with the money you have and the money you'll make isn't something to be ashamed of, although, I wouldn't recommend walking around with a tightwad sticker on your forehead.

Do not let others dictate how you spend your hard earned money. If your neighbor buys a new car, and you still have the perfectly fine 10-year-old model, this is not an excuse to go out and buy another vehicle. Although you may be able to afford such a purchase, consider whether or not you really need another car and more expenses. I'm not trying to give you the starving child in Africa speech to teach responsible financial actions. I want you to always keep it in your mind that you are always one medical disaster or lawsuit from living on the streets. With this in mind, I encourage you to eliminate excessive purchases from your lifestyle. When you pull up to a traffic light in your older car, and that neighbor with the brand new high $$$$$$$ sports car with the leather trim and 10,000,000 HP engine pulls up next to you, keep your head up. Your neighbor puts his or her underwear on the same way you do every morning. The only difference is that you embrace financial responsibility and are not up all night worrying about financial ruin like your neighbor who is swimming in debt. I don't care how strong of a swimmer you think you are; debt water will eventually cause you and possibly your children to drown.

In a material world where the mentality is to have as much as possible and show it off as much as possible, how is it possible to be confident with less? I encourage you to find other likeminded people who embrace responsibility. Hang out with these people. If you are always spending time with those that throw their money away or live lavish lives only to impress their friends, you will likely behave in a similar fashion. Don't write these people off, but hopefully your new-found love for responsibility will rub off on them. The old school mentality of not buying unless you had the money is still out there and much can be learned from this doctrine.

Money can be a slave driver, but you do not have to allow it to have dominion over your life. As I have mentioned before, worrying about money destroys families. What are some ways to turn this around? I wouldn't mention this twice in my book if I didn't think you needed to know it. Talk to your spouse and children about finances. Of course, such matters are confidential, and you should make it clear to your children that it is none of anyone else's business where your family is financially. Don't kill junior if he goes around telling everyone in town that mommy says we have no debt. Although you don't live in a castle, many Americans can only dream of being debt-free. Again I'm not saying it's never appropriate to borrow money, but being debt free encourages you to remain on a responsible track.

Possibly one of the greatest confidence-crushers for the aspiring financially stable family is being too much of a tightwad. Conserving dollars is needed for this plan of financial responsibility to come into play, but cutting into all the comforts of life can lead many to give up the responsible life. You should reward yourself often for being responsible. Remember, you worked for your money, and only you can truly decide the best way to use your money. One does not have to buy off brand food to be financially stable. If I went completely broke someday, I can tell you that I still wouldn't eat anything that comes from one of those dollar store variants. This is my own caveat, and it doesn't have to be yours. Everyone has their own preference for shopping, and as long as you can do so responsibly go shop wherever you want.

If you have done absolutely everything right and still lack the necessary resources to take care of your financial responsibilities, hang in there. In chapters 5-9 I will discuss some part-time endeavors anyone can take on during spare time. I must warn you however, that none of these ventures are a get-rich-scheme. They may not bring you any sort of wealth. These suggestions were chosen because I firmly believe they can be accomplished by anyone regardless of educational experience and these opportunities require little initial capital investment.

Chapter 5 eBay

That is all.

Ever wonder where that slightly used vinyl record from eBay came from? We have all used eBay, but not all of us have sold items on eBay. This chapter is not a sales promo for eBay, but it describes how eBay helped me out in high school, college, and after college.

I went to a rather expensive private college, and considering that my parents were attempting to teach me the value of a dollar, I found myself needing some cash for tuition, books, and the myriad of other expenses that you don't expect, such as that girl who wants to go see the $8 movie instead of the dollar theater special. Oh, wait there is dinner in there somewhere, too, and oh yeah, gas. It is not a cheap time to be a young adult, as I'm sure you already know.

Anyway, I had a collection of antique tractors and parts that accumulated from some of my silly adventures during high school. When I was home from college I took those tractors apart. After disassembling the tractors bolt by bolt, I would begin to take pictures of the individual parts and listed them on the internet on tractor forums and on eBay. Although this method did not write a check to pay for all my loans and every expense that I had, it did provide $3,000-$4,000 extra income for me with little effort or time involved. Again, this isn't like finding gold on the street, but for many reading this book any extra source of income is appreciated.

What if I don't have tractor parts to sell? The great thing about eBay is that you can sell almost anything. At one time I even sold Russian geiger tubes I purchased online from the Ukraine. The bottom line is that we all have junk in our homes and garages that are just collecting dust. Some people make a living buying stuff off of eBay and reselling it. For you, though, I would recommend going out to the garage and filling a box full of stuff you want to get rid of. Take pictures of the individual items and list them online. I think the key to good listing on eBay is that you focus on an item that interests you. If you sell items you are familiar with, after cleaning the shed, you will have an understanding of the market and even estimates in your head of what it takes to ship the item.

How do I get started? Setting up an eBay account is extremely easy. Just go to the website and sign up if you don't already have a buyer's account. Selling is almost as easy as buying since eBay has nice tutorials showing even the most computer illiterate how to sell items. You don't even need a computer anymore to sell your items on eBay. eBay has come out with some really nice mobile apps that allow you to do everything from your phone or tablet. You do not even need a digital camera as the one on your phone or tablet will be just fine. After setting up the eBay account, you will also need to set up a PayPal account, which provides a secure medium for receiving and sending payments. Don't think all these services are free, though. Setting up on eBay and a basic PayPal account doesn't cost anything, but when you make a sale you will have to give a certain percentage of the sale back to eBay just like any other auction in person or electronic. Be careful when selling lower cost items, not to go overboard on the listing pages as quarters here and there can add up. Don't worry, the eBay page will tell you how much your particular listing will cost according to all the bells and whistles on your listing. With a simple but thorough listing, items can be listed for free. You can now add as many pictures as you want now without incurring anymore fees; I wish this had been around when I was younger. Check your email at least daily to see if any potential buyer has any questions about your item. Fast correspondence is one way to ensure that you receive good reviews. It is easy to get started on eBay, and if you are struggling financially, why haven't you tried it yet?

Chapter 6 The Rental Property Model

More than likely you live somewhere. If you don't, I hope things improve for you. Housing is perhaps one of the most misunderstood tools out there. We all require shelter. Because of the Great Recession many have unfortunately defaulted on their home. With this there are about as many foreclosures for sale out there as fish in the sea. Bottom line, houses are cheap right now.

What do you do with a second house? Party? Well, from a business standpoint, I don't want you to marry any secondary housing purchase. The idea would be to do one of two ideas. Probably the easiest idea to grasp is "buy low and sale high." You are probably wondering how a home can be bought at a lower price by you and sold at a higher price to another. Why on earth wouldn't that final buyer buy when the house was cheaper? A couple of reasons can explain this. First of all, I assume that the condition of the foreclosure is not perfect because the home has probably been sitting a while with the grass growing up. This is where a little elbow grease and loving care come into play. Right now, even though the government has pushed large quantities of cash into banks, the banks still seem to be fairly stingy and only lend to those with stellar credit and incomes. This is where your house comes into play.

After doing some handiwork and making sure that the property is fairly clean and most everything works, you can attempt to sell the property yourself or with an agent using owner financing. With this you make an agreement with the purchaser to set up a monthly payment plan, and I'm sure you will want some percentage of money down. You will likely end up charging in the neighborhood of 8%-12% interest because these buyers are probably not going to have stellar credit. I'm not encouraging anyone to take advantage of people by selling your property for WAY more than it is worth. Using owner financing can be beneficial to both parties as you will make money like the bank would and the home buyer gets to make payments toward an actual physical home instead of just sending the money out into the rent vacuum. Often I see people refer to this finance option as a Lease Option to Buy or even a Land Contract. Frequently the house is priced to where the monthly payment comes out about what rent would be for a similar house. When given an option to make constructive payments toward a house or just paying rent, often people will prefer the first. Now bear in mind that there are a multitude of factors that go into making such an investment profitable. This isn't a supplemental income source that I would recommend unless you feel that you are fairly stable in all the areas I discussed in the first four chapters.

The other housing model that many adopt is the rental model. Just about all of us have rented at one time in our lives. We know what it means to be the lessee, but what is it like to be the Landlord? If you are willing to put up with some headaches and are slightly handy this may be a good spare time venture for you.

How does it work? Imagine that people are handing out free houses. Free houses everywhere. Where? How do I get one? Not quite that simple, but it is based upon that idea. When you purchase a house and rent it out, you would have the prospect in mind that the rent you charge is enough to cover the payment of the house, the taxes, repairs, and any other associated costs. The goal is to at least at the very minimum break even each month. When the house is completely paid for, a large portion of the income will be profit.

Why subject yourself to all the headaches involved with being a landlord? Depending on the length of mortgage, if you keep that property occupied, you will have purchased a house and had the renters pay for it. Now, I am going to stop you right there. It isn't that simple, and there are always unintended expenses, renter damages, and the need for a giant bottle of Tylenol. Overall, though, with a little patience and good buying, multiple rentals can provide a decent income especially later in life. It is a fun investment to try at least once. If you are good, you can even use the bank's

money every time and have very little money involved at all

and end up with all these homes that you didn't even pay for.

Average Joe to land baron? That is up to you.

Chapter 7 Part-Time Skilled Labor Market

Skilled labor pays well these days. And if it is a skill that you enjoy, why not put the two together? Sometimes it may feel as if you are just spinning your wheels at work and you don't get compensated as well as you should. Consider one of your hobbies or unused skills and think about how it could become an additional source of income. Take your car to Sears to have the brakes replaced and then invite the air conditioning tech over to fix your AC. It won't take you long to notice your wallet emptying before your eyes. Repairs and services in the 21st century have become astronomically high. Why is this? No one wants to get his or her hands dirty anymore. Personally I think I was born with dirty hands since I have always been working on this or taking apart that, even without permission. My mom and dad sometimes noticed their favorite electronic device did not work anymore, so they would ask me if I knew anything about it. I just ran and hid in my room. You may not be that good with mechanics, but I can certainly tell you that it is never too late to learn.

If finances are tough for you at the moment, consider making some repairs on some household items yourself. These days you can find a guide for fixing just about anything under the sun online. I say this with a word of caution. I don't want any spouses to rage because you accidently turned the blender into a welder. By doing your own repairs you develop an awareness and appreciation of the goods around you. Also, it is educational. If you find something you believe you can become confident working on, perhaps you could turn that skill into valuable dollars. People who are good at things should be compensated for it, right? When I was growing up, I worked on the neighbor's computers, lawn mowers, and cars. You may say to yourself, "I'm not technically or mechanically competent." The reason you struggle with these skills is that you don't sit down and give it a shot. Nothing comes easily for anyone; a little patience and hard work can help anyone pick up marketable job skills.

For those of you who already have a hobby in mind, think about how you will market that skill or product. Word of mouth can often spread like fire. I started doing tax preparation on the side this year, and even though I told no one I was registered to do that, I had so many requests to do taxes it was ridiculous. Of course, I only did a few, as I quickly learned that I despise doing taxes. Word of mouth is a good way to start marketing your part-time skills. You may not be ready to quit your day job, but doing something a few hours a week in the evening can be profitable.

The Internet has also become a wonderful connection for the worker and hobbyist. Whatever your hobby is I guarantee there is a website for it. Learn and connect with these websites since they may produce a valuable source for work. Who knows, you may end up with a job more appealing than your fulltime job. I have a buddy who always worked on mechanical contraptions in his garage when he wasn't working his day job. Now he owns his own shop, offers many services, and works full time doing what he enjoys.

Why are these part-time skills important? As I mentioned in the first chapter, job security is becoming a thing of the past. I hate to say it, but it really is like survival of the fittest. Whatever you can do to increase your marketability will aid in your quest to maintain, find, and also have a backup in case something goes wrong. The problem with hobbyists is that many do not take the time to accurately and proficiently develop what they are working on. To stand out, offer a good or service that is truly of high quality. People do not want poorly executed work or cheap goods, if they did, they would just go to the thrift store for everything or do the work themselves.

Chapter 8 Using Your Computer to Generate Dollars

I have been experimenting with this one as evidenced by your recent book purchase. The Internet has become an important part of our lives, and many, including me, believe there are significant innovations to come in this area. What's great about it is that anyone with a computer can contribute, and that means you.

What if I do not know anything about computers? Too bad, right? I recommend starting out with some type of tablet device such as an iPad or one of the billion Android variants. All you need is something with a browser. With the tablet you can usually have access to your favorite website through mobile applications. After reading chapter 5, you are probably familiar with the eBay mobile application that makes it extremely easy to list all of the stuff you have sitting around your house. The opportunities are endless. Before I continue, I must warn you that this is not a get-rich-guide, and you will have to consult with someone else about that one. All I want you to know in this guide is how to get started in a fashion that will provide supplemental income.

What must you target to make money on the internet? A better question to ask is what it is that you enjoy. Many fail at internet sales because they don't focus on anything in particular, but just try to fire blindly out into space. Pick a hobby or topic on the internet that interests you. For me it is antique tractors. You might not think that anyone interested in that would even be on the Internet or has even stopped using smoke signals. Check out ytmag.com, known as Yesterday's Tractor. It is a massive antique farm equipment site with discussion forums, classifieds, and even an online store. At one point this website was just a little site for Bob and Joe to discuss what carburetor to place on their 1939 John Deere tractor or anything of the sort. Now they have hundreds of thousands of users and an online store that sells anything you could think of in this sector. Bottom line: it won't hurt to try.

You may think that you are not qualified to operate a site of authority on your particular interest. Another great thing about the Internet is that you don't have to have a degree or prove you have a certification in onlinebasketweavingwhilemanagingasitefromsomenationall yrecognizedneverbeenintheclassroomcourse. Anyone can with confidence be an authority online on a matter. Take your interest and make sure you know the basics well. People in the 21st century are interested in sources who have specific knowledge pertaining to some of the strangest things this planet has to offer. If you ever watch some of the reality TV programming, you will be convinced of this. People are interested in the stories and life experiences of others. I'm not saying to exploit these interests. I'm saying that there is a significant opportunity to make a living and help people connect with others through their interests or hobbies.

Ever consider writing a book? You have probably been told that it is extremely expensive and that it takes a walk-on-water miracle to find someone to publish your work. The wonderful blessing of the Internet, though, has opened the door to publishing to almost everyone. However, like the paper publishing business, people are not interested in poorly written or irrelevant work. If you are willing to take the time to compile a truly respectable work, you could potentially make some money. You may not even sell one book, or you may sell thousands. All of this is up to you and your online marketing skills and writing skills.

How do I publish online? You may be reading this text on a tablet or computer. How did it get from me to you? Your purchase was directed through an online store that took a percentage of the sales of this text.. All the big-name book companies have methods for electronic book submission. Some of these sites even provide authors with a free ISBN. There are even some sites that allow you to submit your electronic book in a specific format, and the site will compile your text into the various formats required by the different online stores. The publishing process is not difficult, which allows the author to focus on what is truly important — good content.

Writing books isn't your thing? What about writing software? Learn JAVA, C++, Objective-c or some other common programming language. With a little practice, you could create your own applications and software for computers and mobile devices. This market is relatively new and has much room for progress and development. Application development and programming isn't for everyone since not everyone is wired for it. With a little hard work, though, I believe almost everyone can learn a programming language. It is a matter of effort and confidence. What surprises me is that very few universities require their students to take a programming class. People are often familiar with basic design software, but without fundamental programming skills, their knowledge isn't as useful. The ability to fix that error on the screen is what marks computer competence. Also being able to recognize problems in code can save someone thousands of hours in his lifetime and prevent him from drinking endless quantities of coffee and/or prevent alcoholism from computer strife. People that are truly competent on computers are widely sought-after in this tech job market.

If you haven't taken a formal programming course, don't fear. There are plenty of courses available on a self-study basis through books. In programming, it's helpful to work at your own pace since it requires a good bit of patience. If you stick it out, though, you will not be disappointed. With some programming skills it's possible to make the applications we all love on our smart phones or tablets. There is a certain game I love that involves shooting birds at randomly placed green pigs. You probably have played it yourself. This game is extremely well engineered, and I do not expect you to be able to make anything of the sort. I would recommend beginning with a simple informational app that has some basic tools. Choose something related to your personality or hobbies. What is it that you enjoy or know much about? These topics make it a little easier for you on the creative side of application development. Publishing software is similar to the book process, and I will leave it to you to spend some time on Google figuring the procedure out. Obviously these market platforms will take a percentage of your sales, but this is okay since your application will be accessible to millions of app-thirsty costumers. Again, I must warn you that your app may have zero sales, or it may take off like a gasoline fire. It may even be great enough for some big company to buy you out so you can retire. Do not quit your day job for this. Just keep in mind it could be a good supplemental income for you if you are somewhat computer savvy.

An easy alternative to writing books online or making your own apps is starting a website. Online stores are now incredibly easy to start. Software to build a page isn't even needed anymore since many hosting sites provide web-based design applications. This isn't something most can figure out overnight. It requires some quantity of patience. The website to my financial planning business only took me two hours to build, although it is rather simple in design. Since a lot of people use mobile devices to browse the web, you might want to stay away from complicated designs anyway. Try it; you might like it.

Have good typing skills? Typing can be a good supplemental income because there are about as many keyboarders out there as not. Just in the day of the typewriter where many had to hire others to create documents, such is still the case even in the computer-saturated world of this day. I can recall my grandmother asking me to type up her collection of writings and poetry when I was in high school. Why did she want me to do this? She wouldn't have a computer if it would save the world.

Chapter 9 Hobby Based Income

Ever go to any trade shows? You probably noticed that there are always vendors. While some of these vendors may sell professionally, I'd bet that many are just average Joes who have no desire to sit at a marketplace every day trying to sell junk out of the back of a van like a hobo. Try to find a local show or fair that features an activity related to your hobby. There are shows out there from tree cutting competitions to British car exposé. Your hobby is out there somewhere, and there is potential to make money off of it. In these times every bit of extra cash can help.

I have experience with British cars. I'm going to mention them again. My dad has always enjoyed working on old Triumph TR6s. He also enjoys attending British car shows to hang out with fellow hobbyists. Earlier this year, I gave my dad a flyer about an upcoming show. The flyer mentioned that it only cost five more dollars to register as a vendor, and the fee even included a free T-shirt! We decided to take some extra car parts that were taking up space in his garage and put them in the back of the truck with a clean table and head up to the car show. As soon as we set up, people were crowding around buying these random parts since they were necessary for their restorations. Because of sales from the day and the contacts we gained, we made about $2,000. Plus, now my dad has some more room in his garage.

You can do this as often as you like. My dad is just going to stick to the local shows, which adds up to twice per year. If you like to travel a little, you could fill several of your weekends, especially in the summer. Worst scenario is that you only sell enough to pay for your gas, but you will have some fun meeting other people who appreciate your hobby. Get your family involved, too. Dad is the car hobbyist, but I enjoyed the trip enough that I think I will start working on my own TR6 restoration whenever I finish my other projects...

Chapter 10 The Long Haul

By now you have learned the basics of developing strong finances and supplementing your income. Finances aren't a short game but involve your entire life. I want to retire someday and I would guess that you would like to as well.

If it were not for Social Security, many Americans would not be able to stop working. In these troubled times the existence of Social Security has come into question. Will it be around when I retire? I wouldn't count on it. Although it is very likely that some variant of Social Security will be around 20-30 years from now, I am unwilling to trust my retirement on politicians who seem focused on costly mud-slinging. Assuming Social Security remains intact, it hardly provides enough for most to achieve their preferred standard of living during retirement. With this, we must have some other plan in place to take us to our goal of doing what we want during retirement.

The hindrance to retirement has come from increased expenses for the elderly. Healthy cash flow can be easily consumed. As we get older, we begin to realize that we can no longer survive off of 20 cents of Raman noodles and a vitamin like we could in our younger days. In addition, healthcare costs have risen even with Medicare in place. Planning for retirement begins with determining how much we will need to live our desired lifestyle. Even those who believe they can get by with little expenses in old age are beginning to realize that it can't be done for as little as they planned.

What number are you striving for? Many are blindly throwing money into a retirement account with no plan whatsoever except that they hope to retire at some point in their lives. This is the wrong way to go about retirement. Start the planning process by drawing up a budget that accurately reflects how much your desired lifestyle would cost in today's dollars. After this you need to figure out what that number is in future dollars. With inflation, your money loses its purchasing power, and after 30 years, no one really knows what the dollar will be worth or even if the dollar will still be around. It is always better to put more away than less.

Using US treasuries, for a person to retire with just a $60,000 income without Social Security one would have to have a nest egg approaching the 2 million dollar mark. Let us assume that inflation remains at the 100 year average of around two percent and that the retirement horizon is 30 years away. 3.6 million dollars 30 years from now would have the buying power of 2 million today. There are other factors to keep in mind when considering these numbers, but my point is that it is important to put money away for retirement. There are financial calculator tools available at no charge all over the Internet. If you don't feel comfortable with these calculators, go see a financial planner who focuses on financial plans and charges by the hour rather than by sales or commissions so you can get an objective view of your situation.

The earlier you start saving the better. Easier said than done, right? College drains all of our money in our early years; throughout our twenties we are trying to get our footing and don't have any money; in the thirties, babies start popping out. By the time you are in your forties, you have to worry about sending your child to college. With the mentality that you will begin to save whenever you have money, you will probably never begin to save for retirement. The only way to make it happen is if you make it a requirement in life. Having nice stuff is certainly part of our dreams, but living in a cardboard box when you retire is probably not in this same dream.

Now that you have resolved to start saving for retirement, how do you get started? Payroll or monthly electronic deduction is the best way to go. Those of you who are extremely disciplined are welcome to contribute to your retirement accounts whenever you wish. For everyone else, I recommend automatic withdrawals around payday so that you don't decide to save what is not left over. By saving first, you will have to adjust your budget so that you spend less, which to some is an absolutely profound idea. We have the tendency to put things off until it is too late. Procrastination doesn't work with retirement savings. If you put off saving for retirement, you put off retirement. Many reading this section automatically dismiss the importance of setting aside money every month because they have some sort of pension or defined benefit plan at work that magically guarantees them money during retirement. This is a dangerous route to take. Will that organization be around by retirement time? Even for those with government jobs the recent downgrade of US debt leaves many wondering if our government and its agencies will even hold together. Unless you put away money on your own, you may not have anything at retirement time. If these other sources come through, great. You will have all kinds of cash, but if they don't are you willing to risk pulling out that cardboard box?

Once you have made an effort to start putting money away, you can't just stop there. This is your nest egg, and unless you take care of it, the egg will never hatch. Finding the right investments is just as important as saving. The last ten years have been absolutely stagnant when it comes to just owning the major indices of equities (stocks). The set it and forget it mentality doesn't seem to work anymore as the world seems to be experiencing great growing pains.

A solution to this is called active portfolio management, which involves selecting investments appropriate to timing and performance. Active management is best left in the hands of a professional if you have no idea how the process works. Even though your money is in the hands of a professional, I can tell you first hand that no one has more concern for your money than you do. If you are not spending at least an hour every week analyzing your portfolio situation, you are doomed to failure. America is a great place, but you must make an effort to get ahead. You can choose to be like most people and passively handle your finances, or you can actively take charge to ensure that your interests are taken care of. You can find an entire shelf at most libraries on the topic of investing. Take time to figure out how it works. Your retirement is at stake.

401(k)s, IRAs, SEPs, Social Security, 403(b)s —these are just a few of the confusing terms out there that are either helping you reach your goals or causing you to hit your head against the desk as you read this book. I will cover the mechanics of the 401(k) and the different species of IRAs since these are the most commonly used retirement accounts.

401(k)s are typically used by medium to large sized employers and usually offer some sort of matching percentage as an incentive to put money away. This type of investment is usually referred to as a deferred income plan. The money set aside allows you to decrease your taxable income for the year, but the tradeoff is that when you draw from your nest egg, you will have to pay ordinary income tax on those disbursements made during retirement. Not to sound cynical, but no one knows what those tax rates will be next year, so how are we to even know what the rates will be 30 years from now? If you have some book from the future with this info, I would really appreciate it if you would let me borrow it. 401(k)s are great, and you should take advantage of the most you can out of employer matching. The biggest problem I see with 401(k)s is that employers and employees are often oblivious to what is in these funds and who is managing the money. You should carefully study the history and past performance of your company's 401(k) and the asset management fees that are being assessed. If you find that they are lousy, bring it up with your employer. Not only could you save your chance at retirement, but also you are hooking up everyone else at work. Trust me, people are passive and typically don't look at this in much detail. Your boss will probably welcome your input since his or her money is usually at stake as well. For more information than you could ever possibly assimilate, please see IRS publications 560, 575, and I'm sure there are more as we know the government has to make things as complicated as humanly possible.

IRA or individual retirement account or individual retirement arrangement if you prefer the IRS jargon is an extremely useful tool. The common types of IRAs are Traditional and Roth. The Traditional IRA behaves similarly to the typical 401(k) and allows you to save while reducing taxable income for the year. All growth and savings will be taxed during retirement at income tax rates. The Roth account allows you to contribute using the money you already paid taxes on, and during retirement you don't have to pay taxes on what is withdrawn. This is a great model because it allows your account to grow tax-free. Not only do you not have to pay income tax on disbursements during retirement all of the interest or growth in the account can be withdrawn without paying any taxes at retirement. This type of account is great, especially if you are really good at making money and dislike paying taxes on the gains of your effort.

For more information than you could ever desire on IRAs please see IRS Publication 590.

Interest Rates! What's the deal with this? Imagine that your good and trusty best buddy calls you up and asks to borrow some money. You are close to this person, so you lend him or her $100 bucks. In fact, you trust them so much you don't even charge him or her any interest. The next day word would get out that you are supposedly lending money to any Joe. As these not-so-certain clients approach you, you will probably be concerned about whether or not you are going to get your money back. You decide that the riskier the loan is the more interest you will charge. This, ladies and gentlemen, is how it works in the real world. Interest is basically the price people and organizations are willing to lend their money for. Borrowing money and lending can be drastically different depending on interest rates.

Despite a recent downgrade on US debt, don't let anyone fool you that US debt isn't the most trustworthy investment on this planet. US debt is in such demand (as we often call a flight to quality in the financial field) interest rates have been pushed extremely low. Not only this, short term rates have been kept low as the Fed attempts to stabilize the economy during these unsettling times. For a person nearing retirement or in retirement, this is absolutely devastating because for many, income is directly related to yield from treasuries.

With low rates, though, it is an opportune time to borrow and lock in historic low rates. If you are in a stable enough position to purchase a home, there isn't a better time to get a good loan rate. Although banks have been infused with more money than ever from the Fed through treasury buy backs, it seems that they are unwilling to loan to anyone except the most credit-worthy consumers. They are a bank; isn't loaning money their business? After the housing bust when banks ended up with baskets full of foreclosures, everyone is taking a little bit more care to ensure that people are loan material. In terms of personal financial responsibility, this is a great thing. If you can't get a loan from the bank, you probably have no business buying the property. Even if you can, it doesn't necessarily mean that such a purchase is a good idea.

Continuing this interest rate discourse, I must refer back to credit cards. Just as low rates can aid in making purchases, high rates can stop your dreams of retirement before you even wake up. Credit cards as a whole do not set rates anywhere near housing lending rates. Take a look at your last statement. For many it isn't uncommon to see a rate above 20%. If you are saving for retirement and making a generous 10% on your money, but you are pouring 20% back out to the card companies, which way you are going? Get rid of the cards (rather get rid of the balance; you can keep the cards) at an early age if possible and don't ever resort to racking up a tab on them. I don't care if it is an emergency; all these do is dig a big hole that will eventually bury you and your family.

What does it mean to have a diversified portfolio? This is analogous to having all your eggs in one basket. Let us say as a child your mother sends you to the grocery store to pick up two cartons of eggs. You have the option of carrying both cartons in the same paper or plastic bag, or you can elect to place each carton in its own bag and carry one bag in each arm. As you make your journey back home, a giant dog on a leash sticks its head out of a bush and scares you enough that you drop one of your bags. All the eggs in this bag are destroyed, and then you have to come up with some super awesome excuse for your mother. Now, if you had all the eggs in one bag, you might be crying at this point because there was a good chance you lost all of the eggs. Diversification works in a similar fashion. You need to spread risk out into as many different securities and asset classes so that in the event that something goes wrong with one investment, it will not destroy your entire portfolio. I think the term "security" used in reference to stocks and bonds is rather misleading. Thinking you're secure with any particular stock or bond is rather dangerous.

A common mistake is created all the time when people rack up a large percentage of what they own in their own company stock. This is an accident waiting to happen. I don't care how good a record a company has that does not mean it will continue. By keeping your money in company stock, you expose yourself to twice as much risk. Why? Let us say that things get sour and you get laid off or fired. In addition to this, the stock falls through the floor. You are jobless, and you lost your retirement funds at the same time. Don't fall into this trap, and don't let your company pride interfere with good investment sense.

Where should my money be placed for retirement? The answer to this question depends on the time horizon to retirement and will always be changing as you near retirement. Most financial professionals will interview you to determine your investment goals and objectives. For the most part, when starting early, a portfolio can consist of a high percentage of stocks since this is considered the growth phase, and there is plenty of time to recover from downturns. As you get closer to retirement, it is believed that a larger portion of your portfolio should consist of debentures (bonds or other debt instruments). Speak with your financial planner or advisor. The biggest thing is making sure that you keep an active eye on your investments. It is your money, and if you feel that you have an investment that isn't meeting your expectations, do something about it. The only way to reach your retirement goal is to stay on top of it and do your homework.

You have now heard everything you need to not only take care of your finances but also to build a financial fortress. I encourage you to take these recommendations to heart and above all, start taking an active role in your life and in your family.

www.ingramcontent.com/pod-product-compliance
Lightning Source LLC
Chambersburg PA
CBHW032014190326
41520CB00007B/476